HPS 9839

T0081445

STEVE REICH
DUET

For Two Solo Violins and String Ensemble
or
String Orchestra

HENDON MUSIC

BOOSEY & HAWKES

DISTRIBUTED BY
HAL•LEONARD®
7777 W. BLUEMOUND RD. P.O. BOX 13819 MILWAUKEE, WI 53213

www.boosey.com
www.halleonard.com

World premiere took place on August 8, 1995
at the Gstaad Festival, Gstaad
Performed by Gstaad Festival Ensemble
and Yehudi Menuhin, OM KBE

Duet was composed in 1994 and is dedicated to Yehudi Menuhin and to those ideals of international understanding which Sir Yehudi has practiced throughout his life. The piece is approximately five minutes in length. It is scored for two solo violins and a small group of violas, celli, and bass. Beginning and ending in F the music is built around simple unison canons between the two violins who, from time to time, slightly vary the rhythmic distance between their two voices.

INSTRUMENTATION

2 solo Violins
4 Violas
3 Violoncellos
Contrabass

or

Small String Orchestra

Duration: 5 minutes

D U E T

Steve Reich
(1993)

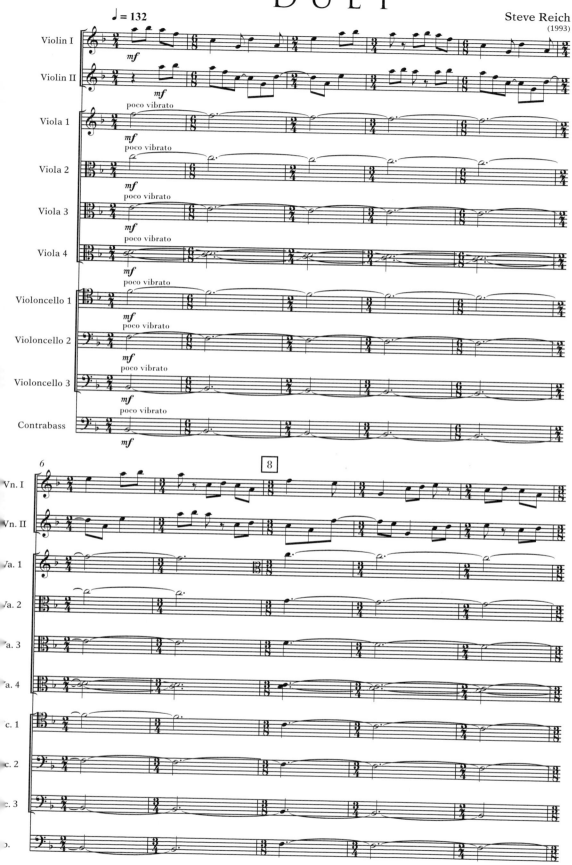

979-0-051-09839-2

First printed 2019
Printed in USA

3

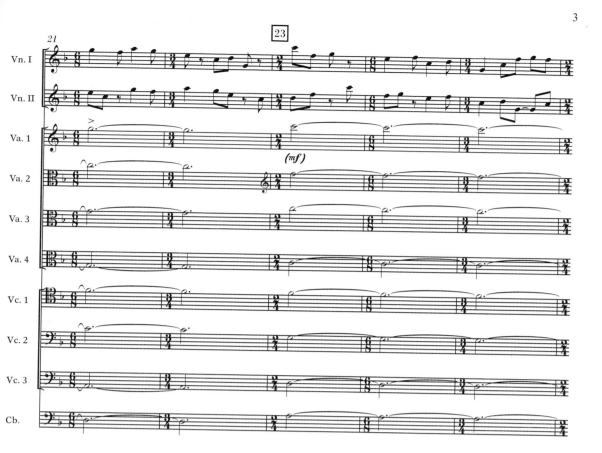

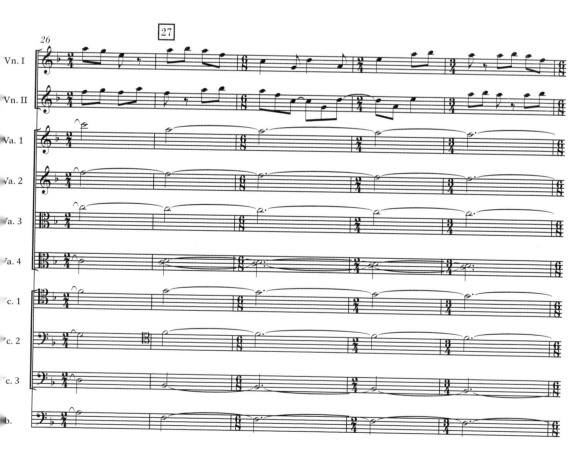

5

brush - (between on & off the string)

12

13

14

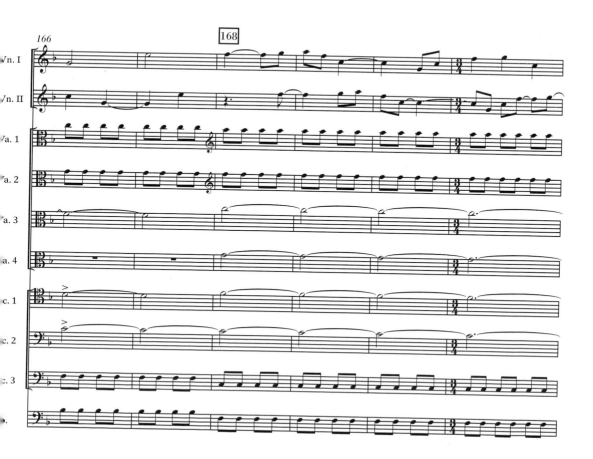

18

20

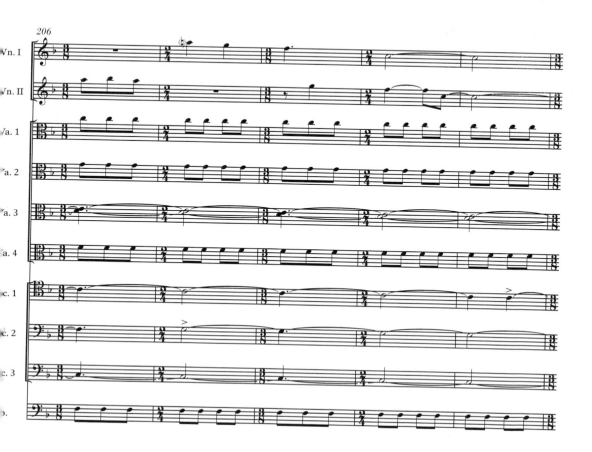

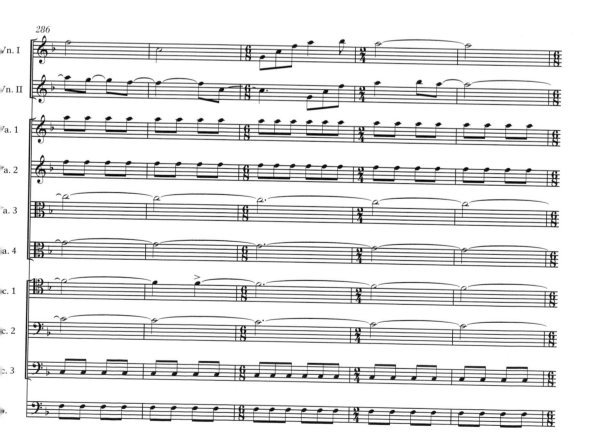

30

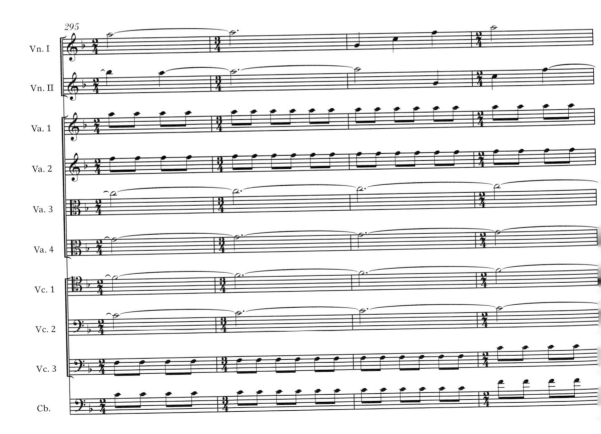